T0394747

What's Going on When It's STORMY

by Noah Leatherland

Minneapolis, Minnesota

Credits

Images are courtesy of Shutterstock.com. With thanks to Getty Images, Thinkstock Photo, and iStockphoto. Cover – MeSamong, ilnazgilov, Artistic Design 24, Technicsorn Stocker. Texture throughout – MeSamong. 4–5 – Torychemistry, justkgoomm, Gwens Graphic Studio, cacio murilo de vasconcelos. 6–7 – Pictureguy, Flystock, Natalllenka.m. 8–9 – Alexpopov, Roman Mikhailiuk. 10–11 – Timodaddy, Pau Buera, Dark Moon Pictures. 12–13 – Fernando Astasio Avila, Nikolay Zaborskikh, Anatolir, BradNYC. 14–15 – Sezamnet, New Africa, HappyPictures. 16–17 – Minerva Studio, Todd Shoemake. 18–19 – Ryan DeBerardinis, Artsiom P, 1Arts. 20–21 – Joko P, Menno van der Haven, robuart. 22–23 – George Trumpeter, Cammie Czuchnicki, kiankhoon.

Bearport Publishing Company Product Development Team

Publisher: Jen Jenson; Director of Product Development: Spencer Brinker; Managing Editor: Allison Juda; Editor: Cole Nelson; Associate Editor: Naomi Reich; Associate Editor: Tiana Tran; Art Director: Colin O'Dea; Designer: Kim Jones; Designer: Kayla Eggert; Product Development Specialist: Owen Hamlin

Library of Congress Cataloging-in-Publication Data is available at www.loc.gov or upon request from the publisher.

ISBN: 979-8-89232-872-2 (hardcover)
ISBN: 979-8-89232-958-3 (paperback)
ISBN: 979-8-89232-902-6 (ebook)

© 2025 BookLife Publishing
This edition is published by arrangement with BookLife Publishing.

North American adaptations © 2025 Bearport Publishing Company. All rights reserved. No part of this publication may be reproduced in whole or in part, stored in any retrieval system, or transmitted in any form or by any means, electronic, mechanical, photocopying, recording, or otherwise, without written permission from the publisher.

For more information, write to Bearport Publishing, 5357 Penn Avenue South, Minneapolis, MN 55419.

CONTENTS

What Is Weather? 4
What Is a Storm? 6
Helpful Storms 8
Thunderstorms 10
Lightning.......................12
Thunder 14
Tornadoes 16
Hurricanes....................18
Staying Safe 20
Stormy Days 22
Glossary 24
Index...........................24

WHAT IS WEATHER?

Weather is what it is like outside. The weather is always changing.

Many things can affect the weather. Storms can bring rain and strong winds. Some even leave behind rainbows.

WHAT'S GOING ON WHEN IT GETS STORMY?

WHAT IS A STORM?

Storms are a type of **extreme** weather. Weather can change a lot during a storm.

There are many kinds of storms. Some storms bring rain and lightning. Others bring strong winds.

HELPFUL STORMS

Storms can be useful. Thunderstorms bring lots of rain. Rain helps cool the air.

Rain also gives water to plants that need it. This helps farmers grow food.

THUNDERSTORMS

Thunderstorms start when it is warm and **humid**. Water **droplets** in the air rise. They gather into clouds.

Water droplets in the clouds freeze into ice. These droplets bump together and make **energy**. This energy turns into lightning.

11

LIGHTNING

Lightning is an electric shock from a cloud.

Some lightning stays in the clouds. Other lightning hits the ground.

LIGHTNING ROD

Lightning often hits trees and metal objects. Some buildings have metal rods. Lightning hits the rod and not the building.

THUNDER

Lightning makes the air very hot. It moves the air around it. This makes the sound of **thunder**.

Light moves much faster than sound. That means you will always see lightning before you hear thunder.

TORNADOES

Storms often bring strong winds. Winds that are blowing in a circle can form a tornado.

16

Tornadoes are tubes of spinning air. Their winds are very strong. They can pick up cars or break buildings.

17

HURRICANES

Hurricanes are storms that start over oceans and **coasts**. Hurricanes spin like tornadoes. But they are much bigger.

The middle of a hurricane is called the eye. There is no wind inside this part. But there are very strong winds around it.

EYE OF THE STORM

19

STAYING SAFE

Some scientists can **predict** when storms are coming. They send out warnings about big storms.

Get indoors to stay dry. Being inside can also help you stay safe from wind and lightning.

STORMY DAYS

Rainy days may keep you inside. But you can still have lots of fun. Stormy days are good for reading or playing games indoors.

Look outside after a storm is over. There might be a rainbow!

GLOSSARY

coasts areas where land meets ocean

droplets tiny drops of liquid, such as water

energy a type of power, such as light or heat

extreme far beyond what is normal or expected

humid when the air has a lot of water in it

predict to make a guess about something that could happen

thunder a loud sound that comes from storms

INDEX

clouds 10–12
ice 11
lightning 7, 11–15, 21
oceans 18

rain 5, 7–9, 22
thunder 14–15
trees 13
wind 5, 7, 16–17, 19, 21